Starters

Salads

Seafood

Pastas & Rice

PASTA

Meat

1 egg   Pinch of salt

150g confectioner's (icing) sugar

420g all-purpose flour

200g unsalted butter

teaspoon of vanilla extract

Directions

Cream together butter and sugar. Add the egg and vanilla extract and mix well. Sift together flour and salt. Add to wet mixture little by little untill well incorporated. Roll, emboss and cut cookies.

Bake cookies at 180°C for 8-10 minutes until tops appear dry rather than shiny.

Secrent is to preheat the oven, and apply the right amount of pressure on the dough

Hints for the Perfect Cookies

Results will be most visible on very thin dough, approximately 0.5 cm in thickness.
Before you press the design on the dough put some flour on it — that way the rolling pin won't stick to the dough.
You can also sprinkle the rolling pin with some powdered sugar — use a brush.
Don't hesitate to press firmly with the rolling pin.
Is the design pressed the way you wanted it to be?
Great!
Now use the cookie cutter to cut individual cookies.
The only thing left to do is to bake your cookies.